# Mighty Machines
# BIKES

Ian Graham

FIREFLY BOOKS

# A FIREFLY BOOK

Published by Firefly Books Ltd. 2017

First printing

**Publisher Cataloging-in-Publication Data (U.S.)**

A CIP record for this title is available from the Library of Congress

**Library and Archives Canada Cataloguing in Publication**

A CIP record for this title is available from Library and Archives Canada

Published in the United States by
Firefly Books (U.S.) Inc.
P.O. Box 1338, Ellicott Station
Buffalo, New York 14205

Published in Canada by
Firefly Books Ltd.
50 Staples Avenue, Unit 1
Richmond Hill, Ontario L4B 0A7

Printed in China

**Author** Ian Graham
**Designers** Phil and Traci Morash
**Editor** Paul Manning
**Picture Researcher** Claudia Tate

**Publisher** Steve Evans
**Creative Director** Zeta Davies

**Picture credits** (t = top, b = bottom, c = center, l = left, r = right, FC = front cover, BC = back cover)
**Alamy** Eric Nathan 14, Steve Hamblin 15
**Corbis** Leo Mason 7, Marvy! 10, Richard H Cohen 18, Tim de Waele 19, Anthony West 22bc
**Ridgeback** 4
**Shutterstock** Digitalsport-photoagency FC, Marcel Jancovic 1, Cornel Achirei 5, Tom Richards 8, Keith Robinson 9, Maxim Petrichuk 11, 16, Ravshan Mirzaitov 12, Lucian Coman 13, Max Blain 17, Timothy Large 20, 21, Anthony Hall, 22br

Words in **bold** can be found in the glossary on page 23.

# Contents

# What is a bike?

Bikes are a useful way to travel around. Most bikes have two wheels that move when the rider pushes down on the pedals. A motorcycle has an engine. It can go much faster than a pedal bike.

Pushing the pedals turns the back wheel and makes the bike move. Squeezing the brake handles makes the bike stop.

**brake handles**

**pedal**

There are all sorts of different motorcycles. Sports bikes and racing motorcycles are fast. **Trail** bikes are for riding off-road, on dirt tracks.

A motorcycle's engine sits under the seat in the middle of a strong frame called the chassis. A chain linked to the engine drives the back wheel.

# Superbikes

A superbike is a light sports motorcycle with an incredibly powerful engine to give it extra zip. Superbikes are among the fastest cycles on the road.

Motorcycle racing is a really popular sport. Motorcycle races can be held on road tracks, special racing circuits, or off-road.

To go around corners at speed, superbike riders lean over until they almost touch the ground.

# Motocross

Motocross races are held on hilly dirt tracks full of **obstacles** and jumps. The motorcycles have knobbly **tires** to grip the track.

Riders must think fast to work out the quickest way around the track. They need to be fit to take part, so they train hard.

Motocross riders jump high into the air on their bike. They can be injured if they are thrown off the bike at high speed.

Motocross bikes need good **suspension** and springy wheels to cushion them against bumps and jolts.

# Easy riders

Harley-Davidsons are big, powerful motorcycles with lots of shiny **chrome**. They are heavy bikes, made for sitting back and cruising along the open road.

Some owners **customize** their bikes by adding extra chrome fittings and high handlebars. These bikes are sometimes called choppers, because their owners chop off the parts they do not need.

The Harley-Davidson's **exhaust** is famous for the deep, throaty roar it makes!

**exhaust**

Many police forces use Harley-Davidson motorcycles because they are fast, yet also good for weaving in and out of **traffic**.

# Four wheelers

A four wheeler is a motorcycle with four wide wheels. It is useful for moving across soft or muddy ground without getting stuck. Many farmers use four wheelers to get around their land.

At quad sports events, riders race their bikes over all kinds of ground, from snow and ice to beaches and sandy desert.

This farmer is using a four wheeler to help round up a flock of sheep.

Most four wheelers have four-wheel drive. The engine drives all four wheels. This helps the wheels to keep a grip on rough or bumpy ground.